n
i
p
m
c
v
t
n
a
q
o
r
v

A DORLING KINDERSLEY BOOK

Devised by Claire Watts
Illustrated by Graham Corbett

Editor Stella Love
Designer Adrienne Hutchinson
Managing Editor Jane Yorke
Senior Art Editor Chris Scollen

First published in Great Britain in 1995
by Dorling Kindersley Limited
9 Henrietta Street, London WC2E 8PS

A CIP catalogue record for this book is available from the British Library

ISBN 0-7513-5361-2

Reproduced by Bright Arts, Hong Kong
Printed and bound in Italy by L.E.G.O.

The Teddy Bear ABC

DORLING KINDERSLEY
London • New York • Stuttgart

opqrstuvwxyz

Aa is for apple, ants, and Adele,

Bb is for Bruno, butterfly, and bell.

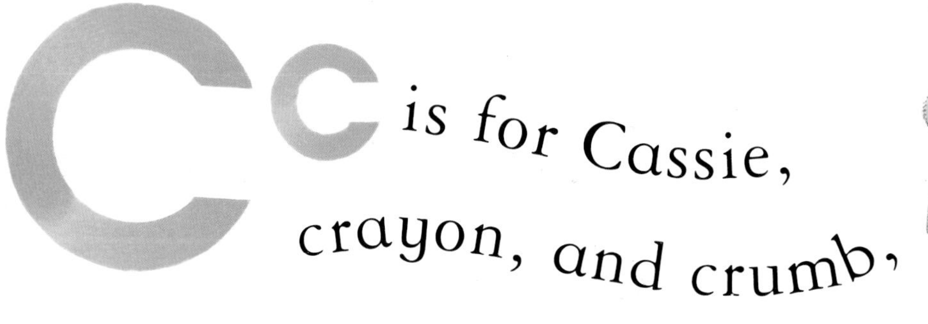

Cc is for Cassie, crayon, and crumb,

Dd is for donkey, Dudley, and drum.

donkey

Dudley

drum

Ee is for elephant, earrings, and Eddie,

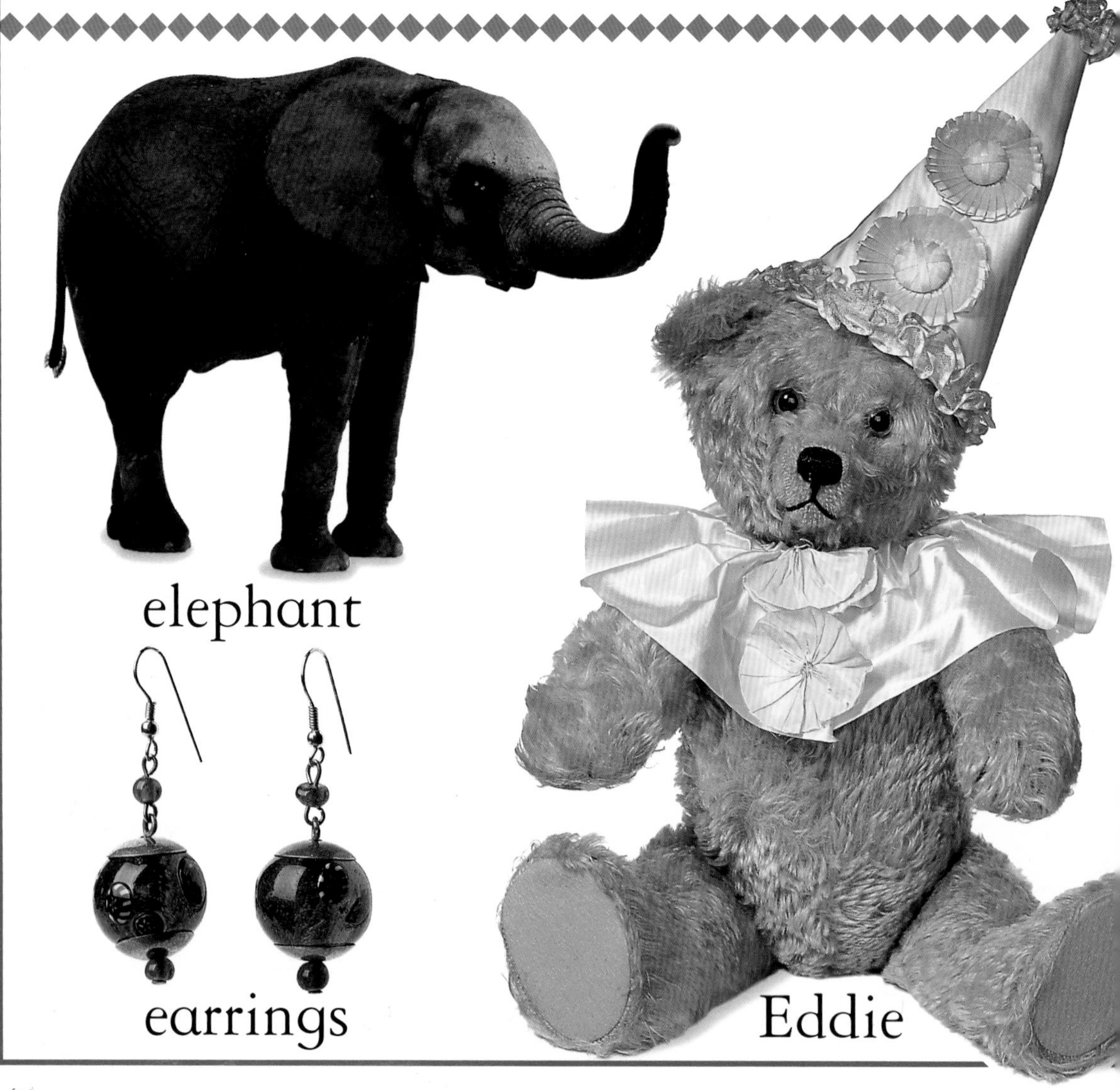

elephant

earrings

Eddie

Ff is for feather, flower, and Freddie.

Gg is for Gertie,
goldfish, and glue,

goldfish
Gertie
glue

Hh is for hat, honey, and Hugh.

hat

honey

Hugh

Ii is for Ivan,
Jj is for Jerry,
Ivan
Jerry

Kk is for kangaroo, koala, and Kerry.

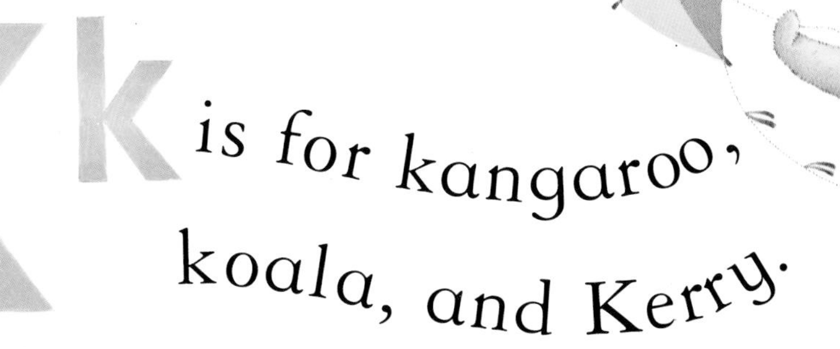

L l is for Luke, lion, and lily,

lion

Luke

lily

Mm is for mouse, marbles, and Milly.

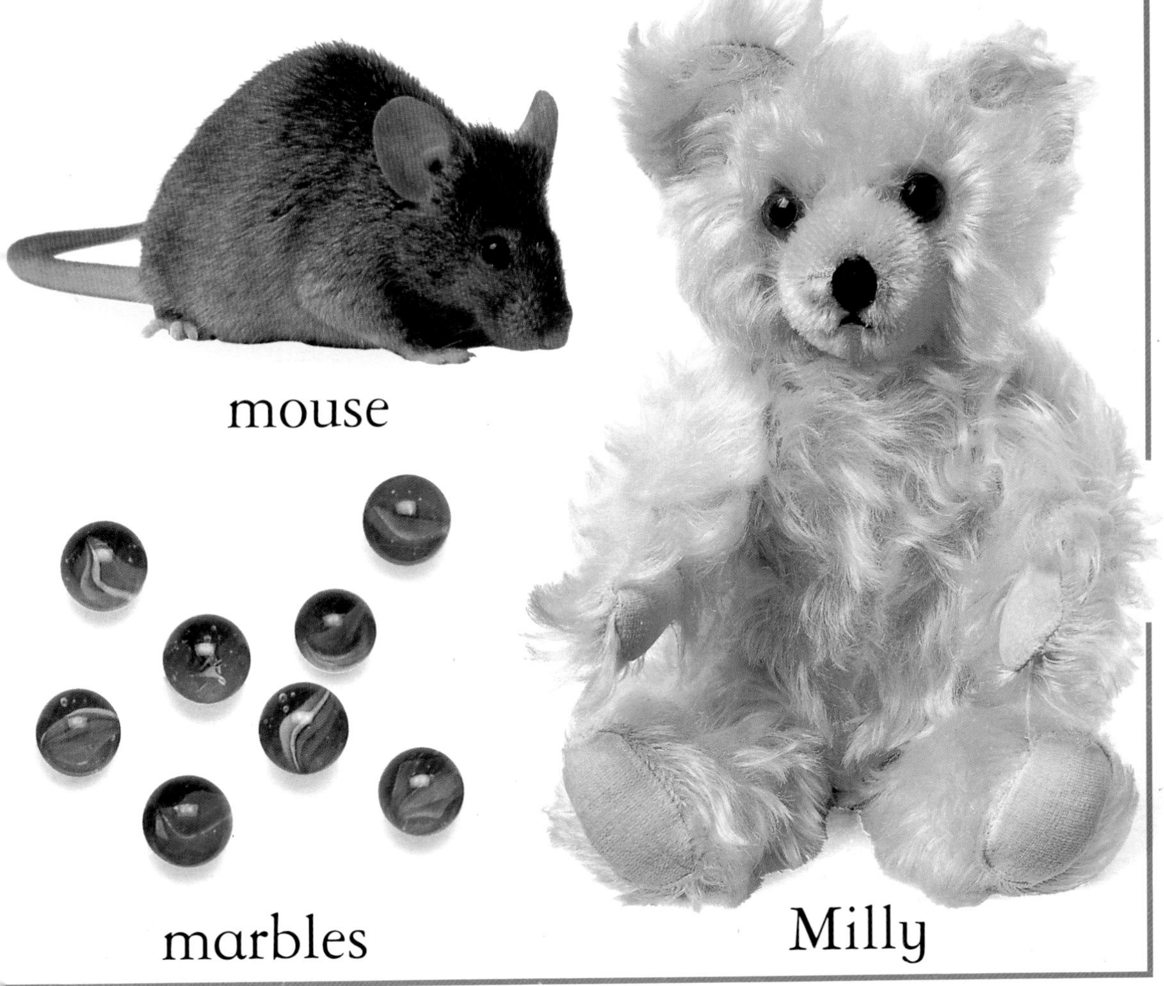

mouse

marbles

Milly

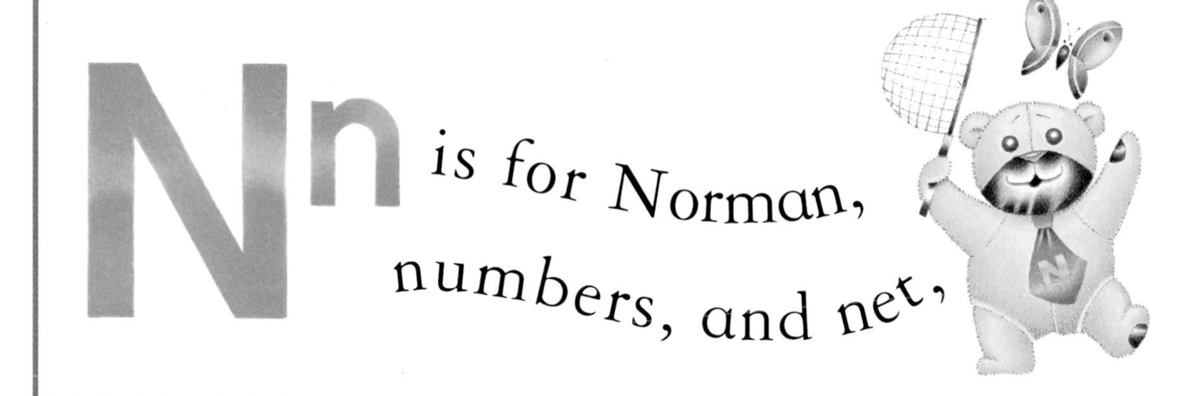

Nn is for Norman, numbers, and net,

numbers

net

Norman

O o is for oranges, owl, and Odette.

oranges

owl

Odette

Pp is for paint, penguin, and Phil,

paint

penguin

Phil

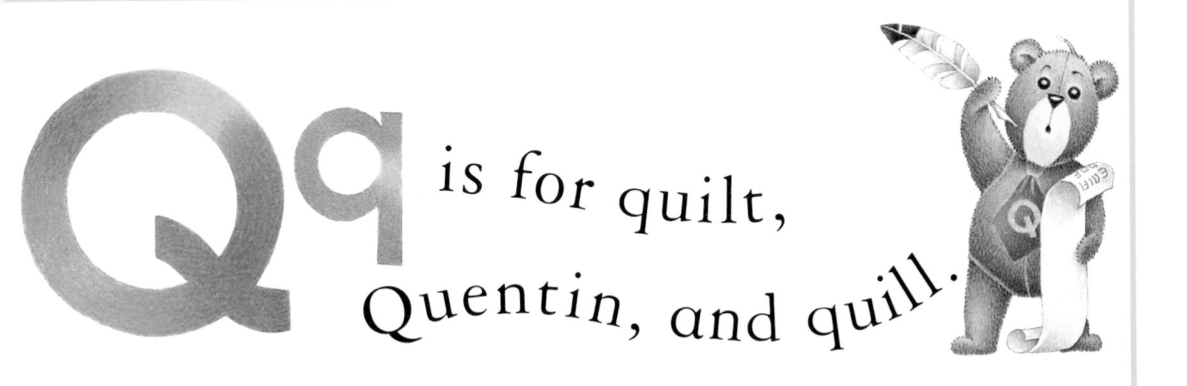

Qq is for quilt, Quentin, and quill.

Rr is for Rory, rabbit, and rope,

rabbit

Rory

rope

S s is for Sarah, sandcastle, and soap.

sandcastle

Sarah

soap

Tt is for Toby, trumpet, and thorn,

Uu is for Ulysses, and unicorn.

unicorn

Ulysses

Vv is for Victor,
violin, and veil,
violin
veil
Victor

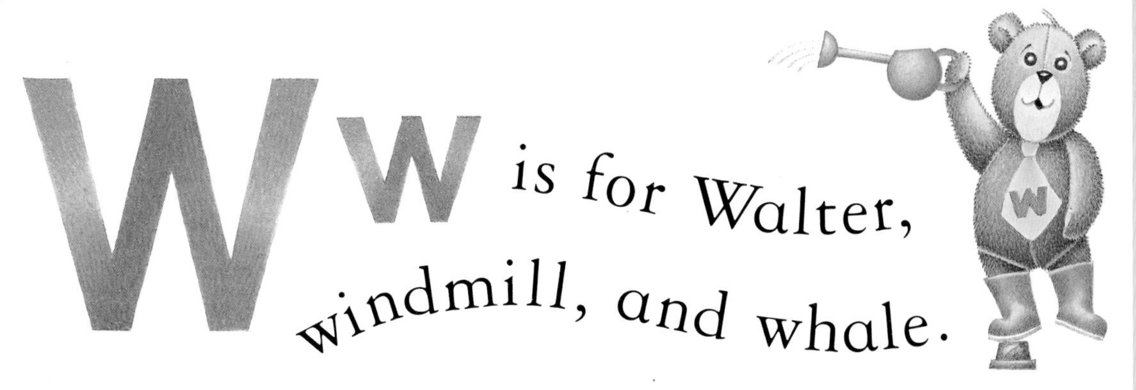

Ww is for Walter, windmill, and whale.

Xx is for Xavier,
Yy is for Yo,
Xavier
Yo

Zz is for zip, Zak, and zero.

zip

Zak

zero

w
b
s
k
f
g
e
x
u
j
l
z
a